T0085824

I am the dead, who, you take care of me

Anthony McCann

I am the dead, who, you take care of me

Wave Books
Seattle/New York

Published by Wave Books

www.wavepoetry.com

Copyright © 2023 by Anthony McCann

All rights reserved

Wave Books titles are distributed to the trade by

Consortium Book Sales and Distribution

Phone: 800-283-3572 / SAN 631-760X

Library of Congress Cataloging-in-Publication Data

Names: McCann, Anthony, author.

Title: I am the dead, who, you take care of me / Anthony McCann.

Description: First edition. | Seattle : Wave Books, [2023]

Identifiers: LCCN 2023009904 | ISBN 9781950268887 (paperback)

Subjects: LCGFT: Poetry.

Classification: LCC PS3613.C3453 I14 2023 | DDC 811/.6—dc23/eng/20230303

LC record available at https://lccn.loc.gov/2023009904

Designed by Crisis

Printed in the United States of America

9 8 7 6 5 4 3 2 1

First Edition

Wave Books 113

But All This

Calamus

Shadow Train for John Samuelson

But All This

Deseret for John Ashbery

Out here someone else is thinking of you,
turning now towards you, to the west
and away. Your table has been set—and that's scary, why not?
But the nominations have begun and soon you'll substitute yourself

in doorways, and on stairs
when these hillsides burst in flames. It's like
tearing the sky with your nipple and then walking back into the scene,
to the wound in the house, to the sink. Blue clouds

rush on through your skull, in the windows
of blood in your throat. Daylight throbs, just out of reach,
there at the lip of your stumps
while behind you, deep in the house, tools as solemn as kids

reassert themselves in the carpeted light
that sleeps beneath tables and chairs.
This house has been you all along
but soon it's bedtime for vision and sound.

Still, as long as it's there you will want it,
will want to be in it, to see it,
to touch the blue tub and have been.
And so, in the bath (where they'll find you one day,

your own mouth stuffed with cool blood)
you pushed open the window and glazed off into space
filled up with blips and new lanes. The world that you see
is just so nearby; one is almost

always surrounded, so that it is almost perfectly safe
and you can open your eyes and still breathe.
Meanwhile, out here, we listen for your breath
like the bodies in songs where no one is home. It's like

turning with your throat in that memory of the house
when already we're inside touching the coats.
But this, you'll never know, you say turning twice away
and then opening the car so the music all spilled out.

So that nothing, or the land, can whistle, or be said,
now the cars all went away in a blast of seeds and dust.
This excitement leads you again to the house
where you'll find your own head, borrowed in glass,

neglected, transpired and waiting to act,
to greet you again with the holes of your face.
The light flecks on your eyes are like fingers on skin
tracing cloud shapes on backs, as they stretch out and pass.

Let this be our city, weaving the light, in the light,
on our backs, in beds, facing up.

But All This . . .

But all this

(dear reader)
is now *yonder*

up the butte (right up there, glowing, it's the *distance*
                    in   the butte)

but for that your mind were late
    your eyes
  are late and warm

    and no one's really here,
but the persistence.
And it folds.

Shadowlands for Jack Wilson

I.

Population, mogrified:
your bodies, risen up.

Even if I'd wanted.
Even if you're not.

So that what am I to *love* it?
Where folded. Where unseen.

On tidy feet: the rain.
this and this
and *this*

2.

or the day
that's not today

that is the
riven earth   stamped
with squares of light

onto which
you leaked your head   mine own

my bad
cracked head: It's not.

It *will* have been. Today
is not Today.
It *came from*. It's for Them.

3.

But who cares
    who cares (the wind!)
when brought to light and end
at door to land etceteras—
and the doctor turns away?

I don't know how you stand it:
Transparency—or men.
But here's the hunger in it,
and the quiet in the range.

Calamus

"*Calamus cannot exist in the presence of cruelty.*"

"*. . . today is the history we must learn/to desire.*"

"*A sparkly tomb a plated grave / A holy thumb beneath a wave*"

"*It's good to be dead in America*"

Calamus

But I had to help the mountain to save it.
It did not seem to
hospital, or other human waste. See
the sequence I've attached—who touching it

should dream. There was endless parking,
a dribbled-out orange stain,
more waste on brave concrete
where I sting beneath your tree.

But I'm inside someone who is me. Demographically
I'd mean, where no one rides for free.
It doesn't matter if he's dead. Or if he's beautiful
or pain; this is the enclosure

and it burns the mass inside. So that my yes-scored sentences
are as practiced as the trees—
because to amuse yourself this way
is to be permanently real. But this is not for reading, or touching

going forth. Neither, if you will,
for thrusting beneath clothes. Who touching you
would sleep, and thus be carried off.
Often there is nothing. No one but our love.

Calamus

First the belly is translated, then the yellow beak,
the solid evil in the eyes, and the wings
to take you up. Because if we act just right
it is possible enough. If the opening is real

through the bed scene on the screen. But without me
who is there, and to whom does it come home
as you sit writing here to death
hands clasped beneath my breath?

The next possibility was extirpation all en masse,
while the weather gets all puff
with the window and the cops. And later, moving in a swarm
to the hideout overhead, the Mountain,

dipped in fog, loomed throughout your blood.
It is the mind of wind that does this. I stand in awe—and wait.
Beneath the sign *Utopia* in bleak athletic type.
Because by then our feelings had been around a long time

and there's a connection between them
and what happened outdoors. You can weave them both shirts;
you can live for the Sun. These wild rocks
are your brothers. Incredible thoughts.

Calamus

Next we are given over to the words of the host;
a bright bitter laughter, terrycloth masked
as it emerges from the kitchen with Tuesday in its fist.
We're the daughter in this dream, in the car named *Hot Escape*—

but this *poem* deals with *our failure* to die
and how the age still supports it, filling the yard.
It just seeps as it builds, and is washed out to sea,
the old silver sea—which never was here.

And who were we really—just some organized space?
Sequence of tubes that repeated itself? All over the beach
with musick and milk, big mammal eyes
when your partner bit back? But there's no answer now,

it all turns back to stones, a too happy tree,
with more arms than we meant. So next time then
I'll just come back as the Dad, and open the scene, to get still as an egg,
pierced by your star when you see yourself now, at the fridge

where you stare and the password expired. Constant Survivor,
your reach is really back—projected then along all that
substantial life. Because it's the dead are pinned to life—a petroleum based work.
Exalted ossifers. When light came through the Earth.

Calamus

when pressing our hearts together on the dream carpet
in the dream room because death, boss comes in
in sullied t-shirt to yell. It's about to
beginning (but he's come from fucking)

spellbound, enraptured (dirty office fuck). In the
heart-grief is pleasures, but boss is commands:
imposture of gestures as the tableau begins.
(Book an end with this walk. the basin *and* the rocks.)

Then someone shouted. The appearance of this was a bright circle,
somewhat somewhere near the ground,
slowly spreading towards us, traveling that ground.
Therefore that he may raise, the lord will throw you down

where there is no world to make, save the pathos
of each shape—and of the shaping afternoon: it blanks us both both ways.
The shadow of each object could now fall upon its weight
and behave still like a wound

while emptying its Christ, *each* Christ
in blue revolt—fulminant, unskinned—
which gives rise to *total* illness,
more pleasure *and* revenge.

Calamus

At the same time, this accomplishes
our selves as sky so far from the rigors of vacation
it's as if, heedless of personal appearance,
"the world" were disclosing a solid. *Yeah.*

It's as if all space just looked at time
but that that isn't enough. *Who?* Someone in the crippled west.
But poets be like singing couches, like
yoga for the weeds. So that when coming through a field

or down from on the hill, there'd be one of almost everyone
fluorescing in the soil. It's an unknown known *condition,*
this sweet killing between words.
But it's because of its persistence—that you'll see it

tapped as joy. It blows the water from my mouth;
you'd call this fitted to endure? But herein
glides the earth—the mass of it, unspooled.
There's nothing there but feelings

and more distance in the soil. I fed a log
into the fire. You got up and went outside.
To keep on happening forever.
Where people fit and why.

Calamus

But I still wouldn't say it's me who looks up
in everlasting permission or that you've ever returned
where you are a semblance to your skill set and death
as red light touched the tips of the brick predicate. It's

how we ritualized intent: when you're lifted
through the glare—the sullen notes,
the beat, the gusty warning bell,
though we have no right to states, which even now I do

but am likely to repent of anything that stayed. So splotch on,
as you must, blotched illuminated thought, like a clump
of heavy rain that has somehow caught the light. Diverge,
fine spokes of light, and shadowed predicates,

to live it out now with the Absence of Earth.
It's like a jelly made from pain. Anyhow, it's work
to mood me into park where your sentence undulates.
But set out in yellow light

I'm not even all that dead. Quiet eyes—the rest—
it's all the math game gone by tent
to east Oregon: the *past*, a perfect copy of the land.
But with all the panic of the meat; forgive us that you're next.

Calamus

Though I still see you in today
and today against my throat.
It's not a friendship pass: We go there—
we get scrubbed. And launched above the phone

face down with someone else—on a body's feeling lines—
the window with itself. But believe me,
that substrate poured from your own eyes,
and is sung, then raided,

by particulate birds: Mock, mock, mock,
and the house breathes it back
through the sweet stink of food
so you hear its own voice.

It's like the happiness of leaves.
And limbs that bangle down
to love all of space until saint-time expired.
Then it's Photograph Mesa, then Photograph Bluff

with light beside death, all Pleistocene-washed.
Till someone dusts us off.
Someone hurt and mild.
And as often as the clock. Someone who's alive.

Calamus

Which is to say "deliverance" but not for you or I—
that banquet is long finished—which poisoned,
rendered us and dumped you over in my body,
my whole weight pinned to earth

through which tubes this image flows
to your vanishment as breath. It's like blue nighttime
of that day, when the day was just your shirt
with light, cold light and leaves,

where *I* sees water and *You* leaks.
Though I'd hoped to say "your voice"
that wind, its tree and grass
with soft fingers on wet throats, then touching living hands.

Because I want life—but for the living,
each lying on its back, each
stored dry for just this moment
to reconstitute as fact

when we heard a child speaking,
just singing to itself,
and there is this song and lips
and *No Country* in our throats.

Calamus

First you'd sense a frame moving through the dust
like lemon-yellow curtains in a single, contact print.
Second, you hear blood. You're Flower Captain of the block
and the blood trade is your blood

though the years go unenforced.
That song—*its other self*—is your territory's map;
carried in the dark, it repurposes your mouth
by the pretty order of the days, in which we'd both enlist

for the went and unkempt rain
of tomorrowland today. Tomorrowland,
Tomorrowland, Tomorrowland Today:
where the moon slides right to left—and the train

gives off its sound, buttering the earth
while it glitters and bleeds out. Meanwhile,
the mountain is another body in a sack
that the light runs its bones across

and it's a face, to no-one else. You, it's "You":
your eyes, your trans-historicated head.
Killing us   (we want)   that makes
a groin   your hand.

Calamus

Because it's always more carcass, more carcass (in oils)
more room number 12 hunched over the phone
in the sorrow and bullshit of the *endeavor* of life
so you can't liberate yourself or say anything at all.

Still your arms would go along
—as if a face looked out—
from blood through blood to blood
till we're the bodies in the cab,

till it's us you saw leak by, as you lay there
by the road, being stitched into a life:
but by whom?—that form is gone.
So just say it, it's the brain that a body has expulsed,

braided, like a fist sitting shiva with the skull.
The client, of course, is this holy one I meant.
‹insert diagram of health   in partitioned office space›
or what we used to call them: moods

where a bench has been brought out
like the corpses in your poems, sky's phlegmatic help.
Or the city, no people, just weather: *the night!*
Whatever it is, it can't know itself.

Calamus

But in the name of that forgetting old September lit the stones
so that it speaks—or walks all night—
while that venue, it still bleeds
and the happy terror of the seen

can still be dreamt beyond our reach.
Or that's just the way it aches. Land tingles in our cords
beginning at the face it's pulled downward to the groin
to point your shoe at stars—their tidy vanishments

as daylight takes the air and all the doves begin to throb.
Or imagine you're the flower and you watch the flower bloom
so when the flower opens up—that's the coming of your name.
I mean, you watch and feel your coming, and this would be your face.

It's as if we'd filled you up with bees—and your stories, little moans,
float up and out the window, like *wherever, man—you're gone.*
But crosswind comes a time when the self begins to see
so that humiliation comes and settles in the sleeves.

We smiled in that sunlight and groaned through gritted teeth
as that impulse also dies which operated us.
The Community, you said.
Because it is not meat. You, she, he, them. Waking with relief.

Calamus

You must have grave dirt locked in your heart:
it must contains a portion
an emblem *or* a cramp
so that one lunges here by night

where charms affect the field
blanketing the field
with a thin quilt of sound.
Power and the logic of affliction repeat

in the chestbone of the Thing Itself,
so that like a shock through matter,
we exist as results, a rock
dipped in feeling, placed in the sun.

"These stones," we say,
"more stones, it all dawns."
But when you turn around and face me
you are streams of colored light—

but when you turn around and face me
with your animal head,
I am already gone in the Nothing-But-Leaves
sawtoothed and silent, dappled with sin.

Calamus

And then how can I but to the chanting invite
the sunshine—a hiss—to push it all off
and speed off into distance, then smell at the earth—
all the gallop of noon: it yielded life

where loose characters drift in their old winter camps
of wheat, beef and pork—to the haste, and you called.
And of this pressure, the seats and the birds I was born
to be somnambular waste, like nobody's time

of anguish endurance and your brood of tough boys
in oblivion tents, where the sound of tin falls.
It showed you more pastures and rude little men
with steep telegraph hearts

and the light hummed around.
They called it Jackpot Alive—while the charge is maintained
but where does it live and
are you merely "shoved in"? Or do you carry that place

to be predictably clear?
It would be a tedious task, like
the worst town, or the world
of experience told, if you get there at all.

Calamus

If you look on each day as a slave (you squeezer of money).
Don't. But if you don't. But if you left rationalism
and English teaching as if it didn't.
As if radical vagabonds, as if

sleepless on tape, it's like your legs moved a little
and that made no decision. Teaching
was just the teaching of this drink.
Downtown, on the other hand,

was a good place to sit
with luminous globs all over you.
Then the ferry horn, and the hurried passage back.
Then the middle of the harbor,

then the voices flowing back.
The voluptuousness of this extraction
awaits you. It unpacks you, Star Daddy.
But I'm doing the opposite. It's like when I go to college:

continuous sleep. It happens continuous
between me and my skin. So that after 3 seconds
I just let it spill out:
between me and me. Let there be clouds.

Calamus

Today revelation is civil war.
So now I'm rooting mainly for the plot.
Like (fingers asleep) for meaning. Is what he says.
But touching each other in forgiveness

You has not killed *Me* and *We* is consoled.
It's like a belief fence expressing thought densities
or in-kind Disaster Suites.
Because it's right that we be flames.

Because I was the shoulder. But I was the legs.
But you whistled on by
when you whizzed past my head. Less like a thief
than to murder at the word

and run for sheriff of itself—
but the insanity of stars. It just pins you,
it all pins you. As if a great body,
God's ownmost solid cow, had struck

my humble roof and vanished
leaving sound. Historically, I mean,
or *actually*: today. But every time I rush outside,
each time there's nothing there.

Calamus

Rail water at the ankles, says the speaker, is a ghost:
a strand of corpse that's yours,
doubled off the heart. This was further evidenced
from its most numerous feet

and head (that low protuberance)
as if surrounded by no light. More evidence was brief
and it frightened me terrific:
Dogs, smoke colored, at the edge of blue woods. *A boy*

held aloft in terror as in grace.
But then some people gave me coins, a pork sausage
in my suit, and Daddy, it all jingled
like toast and eggs in church.

I wore it next morning
where hair flew out their mouths.
I wore it next morning
And could not (be) believe(d).

But Christ I saw the(m) woods,
and understood that it must night.
Where resting on our haunches
and looking backwards toward the house.

Calamus

Shortly after this, some antennae rustled out
and then hung downward from your body
as if towards the living earth. Next there was a howl, culled out,
and well sustained, mixed with liquid

rising yips from three more persistent throats.
Then you followed with your voice, then came silence,
then the dogs, from just beyond the gate
where the night was very cold.

The next night was starved and wilted,
while mother rode to church
too terrified to look
into the bog of our good luck—

the dark church
taken: a plate of buttered toast
Buttered Toast and starving
so I enjoyed the wide view.

But Daddy, who can stand it?
It all jingles as with wounds
and a nice lake, who is blazing
though I wouldn't know which one.

Calamus

At Easter mother showed the Sun: the dancing, molten joy
the molten globe, and skies. Then,
through nettles and the hedge, I could climb
the whitethorn hills

and roll down into the ditch,
and rise up from the dry drain
and then take more days (and years) to cross
that wheaten sedge mirage

that lay down between two hills
to walk into the Sun. You fell into a sleep.
You heard voices call your name,
then the night went very blue

and could not be observed
by which body that carried it, nettle and briar
through this small wooden gate, as peeled as brains.
This, said the book, though I wouldn't know which one,

shapeless as it was with windows
(as with sound). *A small wooden gate.*
And the cottage abandoned.
And the Doctrine abandoned, which belonged thus to God.

Calamus

This violence had been organized
the people driven south
till they rested right here, and stayed 200 years
in Soft Animal Trespass

with Sycamore Ink—to call out down the lane
when fathers were the law. There was a large
brown bin and three sisters in that room
and a small red lamp

beneath the hologram of God;
the kettle went to boil
while the moon in the small lake
swung out heedlessly through trees

as if we all would never die. But all them names
were northern, the stream
with its small pools, through which many were related
and every house was burned.

All so you could be a priest,
in coats where night had turned
reflecting the pale moon
in the gravel of the road.

Calamus

There was silence for a long time. Parochial rain.
But your shame would be public
before I reached the school. I ran and ran
—the wheels!—in agony for mass

and hung about the land
till hunger dragged us back. Because one day
when you'd all died
I knew *I'd* be the priest

and place my unwrapped hands
in your unity of God, your boggy meadow names
and their seams beneath the earth
running up the slope

through windows in the turf. That mountain was a face,
smashed mouth and lumps of teeth
through all its shifting light
and every child stared.

Till the giant had descended,
come down the mountain in that rain
as now he watched us from the porch
and not one roof was saved.

Calamus

What is my dream? Sitting on the lip
of the world-dark
falling. That is not my dream. You,
riddle me this. Tell me my dream.

Bringing water (voices) in the dark. Water for eyes
to bring lips and throats to see.
That you may look around. That we may look around.
For a little while. That this has been my dream.

I mean the Earth Room. But who goes there
over green hills into light?
Who is it that then goes on into thunder?
Is it You, Green Thunder?

Is it You filling my books? O,
is this yours? O, You, hey
with the corpse in the tree?
O, You, hey. Listen how it speaks:

Gray face and certain
knowledge that it speaks.
That in the dark beside us
it's someone else who dreams.

Calamus

I had gone forth from our village
in my usual manner, in order to groan
more freely before you. You, who are the dead
who I take care of. You,

who the dead take care of me. Here were letters,
pinned to trees
along the forest at the stream
whose images are buttoned

to your flesh when it was peeled. The woods:
the smell of woods. Moss:
the touch of moss,
as each sensing in our story

becomes a providential corpse. Yours,
your missing corpse. It proves
the presence of your name,
in the absence of my throat

where logs turn into loam. So, Little Father, raise it up:
the light's a stone that speaks
made of meat and hair
in your hand where it still bleeds.

Calamus

I call it Consolation when some movement is caused,
Interior Movement where the soul can be inflamed
and love no created thing on the face of Earth itself
(where quite often there is nothing: nowhere but *His Name*).

I'd placed a short prayer within my little box
wherein I asked for violent death
and the grace to shed my blood,
so that then I saw before my eyes

when I removed it from your grasp
my own sentence *in my blood*:
faint mockery of love. In the rain
and mud my chest was stripped of flesh and hair,

and imaged to the bone—all as written, in my hand.
But that's not the way to do it:
I was made instead to sit
and make the dead alive again

in person by their words. In *my* person
by *your* words. It's our almost
favorite scene: the Final Getaway,
floating backwards through the trees.

Calamus

But there are bodies all rejoined,
bodies all at once.
These bodies will surround us.
And shouldn't we be glad?

When the bones connect to bones
when the nerves are each rejoined
when the eyes sweep side to side
as if they came here all at once.

This is what it brings me, desiring it be such,
as if they came from all directions
these bodies all at once.
I say go enter in that tent,

and see your corpse laid down below
and your name with all its *rage*
hanging over it like smoke.
It is *alive*, I mean, the corpse and all the dirt

and corresponds to feelings
that in book-time we'd call *souls*. I mean the data,
Information: all that flesh that you've consumed.
It is not or ever *missing*. But it is not ever yours.

Calamus

This greeting is in my own hand:
This is how I write: Waterless Clouds
blown apart by winds, Shadows
on your feasts of love.

Such had been the purpose
of this, our final gift: to google
search accumulation, apotheosis, adze
and introduce the kingdom

mate the kingdom to each corpse.
But twice dead and then uprooted
off we've gone again—
as each swearing makes light shiver

at the future, where you're young.
Because here behind this rock
there is another rock, with all the bright etceteras
like you've found its secret brain,

the Day's I mean, its dream
of light spread out on dirt,
and a little plant that grows,
whose world will not be named.

Calamus

Or in the tube of the earth with hot flanks of the herd
and what renewals of the moon, so that finally you remained.
There are fools to call this "memory."
There are fools to call it "mind."

When the clouds are peeled back
and light creeps up the hill
your head will be attached
and you will not be wrongly tuned.

Our hearts will hang *here*—
just here between our arms.
We will eat and slowly grow. You will eat, you will go:
a voice, where medicine spreads.

If we cut off your feet, it is there.
If we cut off your hands,
it is there. When juniper. When sage.
When rabbitbrush. When clay.

An animal and our body go together in this matter.
When houses of clay: it goes.
When yellow with houses, when wind.
When yellow with houses, when bones.

Shadow
Train
for John
Samuelson

Shadow Train for John Samuelson

For one long day the city looked for teeth,
for its own shattered teeth, in the desert at its rim
                 and then turned away
stiff-necked, to glare at the ridge

and by that time *No One* was you. The white land
was dipped now in blue: deep blue and light purple rust.
But on the screen we see only your hips
and it seems like the dark never comes.

Or that's the last hit we inhaled
before surrendering hope to the stones.

Caught in that distance was deliberate fear
and then nothing was there
to talk itself through, but still you thought we could hear it
and then see the whole mood

in the glowing rock face, till the sheriffs appeared.
As if the cops hadn't been there, in those
slender walkways
through the outlying space—when you discovered the words

when you discovered events, and the words
that they ate, past here in the dark
with their nerves on display. But that dish has been plated.
We're sorry, we'd said. And then the houses and numbers

were hosed down with light, by the noticing light
in the districts that want. Still sorry, how sorry, so sorry, we said.
But the violence continues
where the blue edges wait. In front of us

footpaths lead down to the tanks. How protected it was!
Unhappened as yet. And down in one corner
where the glass wasn't broke
there was peace in the spines

and the empurpled rocks. Because flesh
is for damage, where movement
meets cramps. Like in heaven,
they said, and the syllables

drained. But we too were thinking
of casting away, and of sunlight and shadow
on the limbs that we'd placed
where we'd touched everything

for pleasure and luck—
with the cacti and bones
in the grooves, with the scrub.
Our catastrophe stayed there

the way that you did
unrolling its map, to never come back.
But a map is a map
so you're already here, at the Mall

of the Desert, you'd never *exist*.
So we turn to each other
there's room in your face
and in the stance of each pole

but where was the past? There aren't enough flares
for each ragged leaf, for the turns
the day took, and the night gathered back. After that
we still might never be friends,

but it's not just about dying
and it vests over time, so that now you're this thing
that just looks like itself,
beneath a sky of red schist

but it's glowing in place. Yes,
you said, thanks, you said, this will be fine
as if I'd said you were there
advancing through light.

Because it is the old meat, no matter how old,
and this is nobody's room,
it's *glory* you meant. But that's not enough really,
and it's really gold spines,

that drill in the flesh, to make you have sound.
Such was our youth, or the beginning of age,
where I puked on your shoes, but we talked until dawn,
until the blue glory rags

were whipping through blood
and over the dust where the grid had been laid.
Male bodies appeared, the sun at their backs, sneaking back
through that park, in the city-wide stench.

And though you're sure I'm not *him*
I've passed into your speech
and entered the bar
over there with the rest. "Contact," you said.

Between fingers and *them*
so my bandage gets ripped
and our wound hits the air.
And doesn't it hurt, everything we forgot,

uncoiled this way,
so the world is your throat? It's *your* body now,
and how written it was, as if covered with eyes
where we lay on the floor. Correction: *la* flor,

as if covered with *ice*
we'd been lifted through sleep,
and the sequence expired. In the meantime
we lived on in your veins,

in the dusty outskirts
where the terminal aches, and the buses start up
in the scent of fried meat,
while the grey film of the road

rolls on underneath. It's a death trip, man,
we've got to show them what you are,
for their symbol *must* continue, and then you're nowhere else.
Correction: *in the wind*, and there were others

dribbled past, as we gnawed along the edge
and sigh now with the force. It's been played again once more,
for all those thirsting ears, each of us,
a cell, quickening through walls—your voice,

another voice, places, times and names
conscious of all life, without knowing
that it lived. You could see it like a word
fullborn already dead, like a sentence,

the whole phrase, lit up like human teeth.
Glorious, whole teeth, that money
could restage, when under neon threads
cool mist has kissed your vents.

Till you thought to go beneath,
below the surface face, of the first
shiver of remembering, out the window
all that day. *That is simply not my name*

said the window to the world
and the figures sliding by, like handles
between men. There was a glint
between the clouds, all along

the stubbled rocks and here
the friends were placed,
imagined in the gulch.
So don't bogart it now,

pass it over here, and let a body
be the rain, on the rocks
all afternoon   in rust

gray mist
and pink   brown
        pink and

orange grey sand. And a scent
of risen up, wet and
rank with limbs. But there weren't nobody there.
Just the creosotes, and stink,

land, the given night,
your belly underfoot. So drink it,
hold it down, let your body
be lit up, in the spoken lights of cars

angled through the pass. No one
can really see you, it's just
your teeth and face, for a second
in the lights and then they don't believe.

So you watched them with your teeth.
A certain distance sampled you,
stained you a bluer blue;
so now it's someone else's way,

someone else's dawn, seeping
over rocks, till the wind, the air,
the roof, everyone is real. The city
stammered back, visible in waves

through blue and yellow dust:
the precedent was *there*. It's like a memory
of food, of ravens, all their wings,
the boxes filled with bones

and so we gather at the curbs.
One foot. Two foot. The City in its Wigs.
And something whistles somewhere
but our permanence begins.

The title of this book is a translation of a mistranslation. The original author of the phrase, 17th century French Jesuit missionary Jean de Brébeuf, meant to say something very different in Wendat, the language of the Wendat (Huron) people of what is now southeastern Ontario. (He was attempting to express the Christian figure of a "guardian angel" in that complex tongue which was famously resistant to many European Christian concepts and cultural and political priorities.) Canadian scholar John L. Steckley has translated de Brébeuf's awkward Wendat into the uncanny English phrase that graces this book's cover. To learn more about Jean de Brébeuf and some of the many other historical and literary figures and sources which traverse this text please go to the book page for *I am the dead, who, you take care of me* at www.wavepoetry.com for additional notes.

Eight of the *Calamus* poems in this book originally appeared in *The Brooklyn Rail*. Thanks to editor Anselm Berrigan. Thanks also to CAConrad for their anthology on Death which included two additional *Calamus* poems. Thanks to the editors of any publications where poems from this book might also come to appear. Thanks to Kirsty Singer and Tomaž Singer-McCann for their sustaining companionship and contributions to this work. (Thanks, Tomaž for your early performances of some of these poems, which helped so much to clarify their voicings and purposes.) Thanks to all involved with Wave Books who helped convey this work into its current public form. I would also like to thank the Mojave Desert, the Great Basin Desert, and the Eastern Woodlands of North America for the life and speech they sustained in me over the years of making these poems.

The epigraphs that open the *Calamus* section are from the following four poets, listed here in the order in which the quotations appear: Jack Spicer, Amiri Baraka, Philip Whalen, Peter Gizzi.